GOPRO HERO 12

USER GUIDE

A SIMPLE USER GUIDE ON HOW TO USE THE GOPRO HERO 12 CAMERA.

ISAAC LEMMINGS

TABLE OF CONTENTS

INTRODUCTION

GoPro 35mm Hero was the first Hero camera that was introduced by GoPro Inc. A Subsequent series of the Hero camera was released, from HERO3+ to HERO6, then to HERO7. The update continued till the recent version of the Hero series was released; GoPro 12 Hero camera.

The newest and best action camera from GoPro is the Hero 12 model. Anyone who wishes to record their activities in high-quality video and images should choose the GoPro Hero 12. It is ideal for everyone—athletes, tourists, and regular folks.

The GoPro 12 Hero camera has a new GP2 processor that enables it to record 5.3K video at 60 frames per second and 4K video at 120 frames per second. Additionally, it includes a brand-new 1/1.9-inch sensor with a greater dynamic range and better low-light performance.

In this user guide, you will be exposed to how to effectively use the GoPro 12 Hero Camera whether as a novice or as an expert, its parts and how they work, basic and advanced operations to carry out with the camera, and how to effortlessly use the device for any function, event, and territory.

CHAPTER ONE

INTRODUCING GOPRO HERO 12

Go Pro Hero 12 Black is the latest product of the GoPro line of action cameras that comes with more friendly features, including a new sensor that allows users to create vertical videos for social media platforms such as TikTok, Facebook, etc.

This device is accompanied by a nearly square 8:7 chip and a camera with a resolution of 5.3k recording options that allow creators to cut landscape and vertical videos from the same take.

GoPro Hero 12 is embedded with the latest video stabilization technology. With HyperSmooth 5.0 features, AutoBoost, and Horizon Lock built-in, creators can take smooth and stunning shots.

WHAT'S NEW ABOUT GOPRO HERO 12

The GoPro Hero 12 comes with the following astonishing features that make it different from the previous versions of GoPro Hero:

- **5.3K Video Recording at 60fps**: One of the major and glaring updates that came with Hero 12 is the 5.3k video recording at 60fps. This means that Hero 12 can record 5.3k video at 60 frames per second, thereby giving the video a smoother and more fluid resolution with less motion blur.
- **HyperSmooth Auto Boost 6.0 in all Modes**: Another feature that comes with GoPro Hero 12 is the upgraded HyperSmooth Auto Boost. This feature utilizes both the software and hardware to create smoother and more stable footage by reducing camera shake. In other words, AutoBoost 6.0 maximizes image stabilization while minimizing image cropping.
- **Enhanced Color Depth Using 10-Bit Recording**: This feature allows you to make 10-bit color recordings for finer gradations in your footage. With this feature, more color information can be captured which in return allows for more precise and lively colors in your footage.
- **GP-Log Mode**: Another feature of the GO Pro 12 is its professional recording profile, which gives you a greater advantage or control over how your footage's color and dynamic range are used in post-production.
- **Microphone Support for Bluetooth**: The Go Pro Hero 12 allows you to use wireless microphones which go a long way in providing a quality and better audio performance.

- **Internal 1/4-20 Tripod Mount:** The Go Pro 12 comes with a built-in 1/4 tripod mount. With this mound, Hero 12 can be attached easily to a tripod and other mounting devices.
- **Longer Life Span Battery:** The new Go Pro Hero 12 can record for 70 minutes in .3 in 60fps unlike the Go Pro Hero 11 that lasts for 35 minutes.
- **HDR Video Mode**: This new feature of Go Pro Hero 12 provides your images or videos with a wider range of brightness, colors, and tones, giving them realistic and natural-looking videos.
- **Timecode Syncing**: The device has a timecode syncing feature that allows you to align the timecode of several videos and audios for easier editing during post-production.

THE SYSTEM REQUIREMENT FOR GOPRO HERO 12

To begin to use the GoPro Hero 12 device on your PC, there is a need to download the latest GoPro software on your PC (Windows or Mac). First and Foremost, you will have to visit gopro,com/getstarted to get the software downloaded.

The following are the requirements for the installation of the GoPro Hero 12 on your PC for either Windows or Mac operating system:

	Windows	Mac
Operating System	Windows 10 or later	macOS 10.15.7 or later
CPU	Intel Core i5-6th Gen or AMD Ryzen 5 1600 or later	Intel Core i5-6th Gen or AMD Ryzen 5 1600 or later
Graphics Card	Intel HD Graphics 620 or AMD Radeon RX 550 or later	Intel HD Graphics 620 or AMD Radeon RX 550 or later
Screen Resolution	1366 x 768 or higher	1280 x 800 or higher
RAM	2GB (4GB or greater recommended)	8GB or more
Hard Drive	5400 RPM internal drive (7200 RPM drive or SSD recommended) If external, use USB 3.0 or eSATA	5400 RPM internal drive (7200 RPM drive or SSD recommended) If external, use Thunderbolt, FireWire or USB 3.0
Storage	Nothing less than 10 GB	Nothing less than 10 GB

Note: You will need a strong internet connection for your software updates and cloud storage

CHAPTER TWO

GETTING STARTED WITH GO PRO HERO 12

Here, you will be getting familiar with the basic things you should be able to do with Hero 12. It doesn't matter if you have never been acquainted with the previous versions of Hero 12. Sit back and watch how I get you familiar with the basics of Hero 12.

GETTING FAMILIAR WITH THE BASIC PARTS OF THE GOPRO HERO 12

Before we begin to learn the different functionalities of GoPro Hero 12, it is pertinent that take our time to learn all the basic parts of GoPro Hero 12.

The following are the basic parts of the GoPro Hero 12

- **The Shutter Button/Start Button**: This is the button that allows you to power your camera and start recording. When it is pressed again, the camera will stop recording. With the Shutter button, you can activate quick capture. The Shutter/Start button is located at the top of the GoPro Hero 11 device.

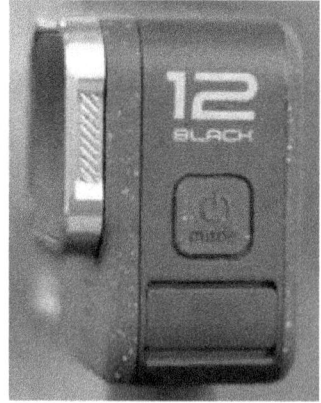

- **Door**: This is located at the top of the camera with a convenient port that allows easy access to the internal parts of the camera and it conceals the microSD card slot and battery compartment. The port opens like a small door and is closed when not in use to prevent dust from entering the camera.

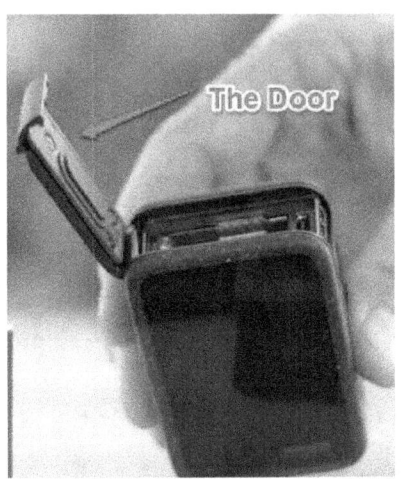

- **The Door Latch**: This is attached to the door in the camera.

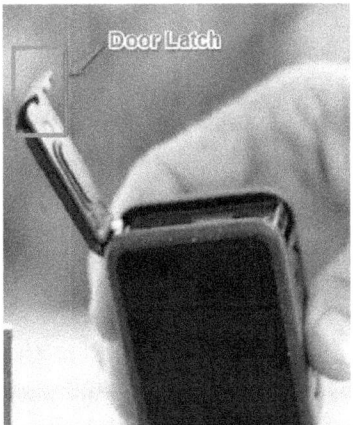

- **Status Light:** This is an LED indicator located at the top of the camera and it is used to know the status of the camera. With the status light, you can check if the camera is recording or doing any other things.

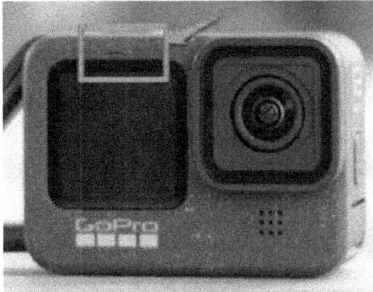

- **Front Screen:** This is one of the features of GoPro Hero 12 that has a full-color live preview screen used for vlogging or selfies.

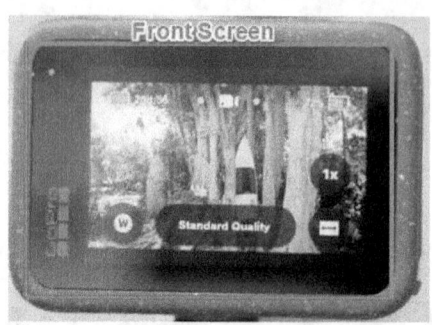

- **MicroSD Card Slot:** This is located beside the battery and this is where the SD card is slotted. The MicroSD card slot is protected and covered by the door.
- **Battery Slot**: This is directly located beside the MicroSD card slot and where the battery is inserted.
- **USB-C Port**: This is the point where the USB charger adaptor is connected to the camera to charge its battery.

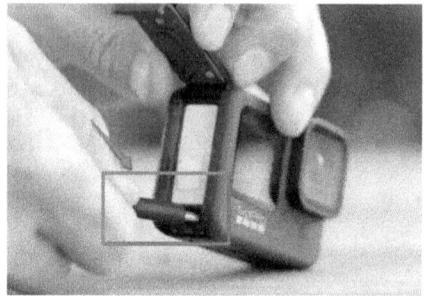

- **Microphone**: You can capture audio using the microphone, which is on the camera's top. It is the part of the camera that helps improve the clarity of dialogue when subjects speak in front of the camera OR capture more natural environmental sounds.

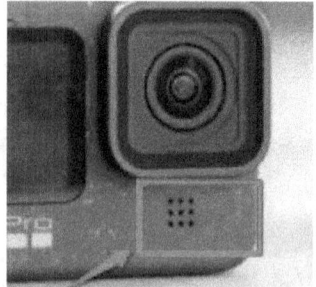

- **Removable lens**: A type of lens that can be detached and replaced in the Hero camera.

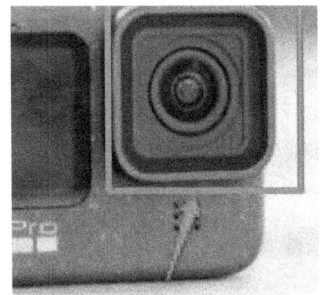

- **Mouthing Fingers**: To install the camera to different mounts and accessories, utilize the mounting fingers that are situated on the bottom of the camera.

The GoPro Hero 12 camera comes with a variety of optional extras in addition to these standard components, including:

- **Light Mod**: This add-on gives the camera a strong LED light, making it perfect for shooting in dimly lit areas.

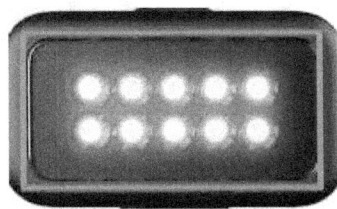

- **Media Mod**: A microphone input, an HDMI port, and more mounting points are all added to the camera with the Media Mod accessory.
- **Max Lens Mod 2.0**: The Max Lens Mod 2.0 is an add-on that gives the camera a 155-degree field of vision, enabling it to take incredibly wide-angle photos.

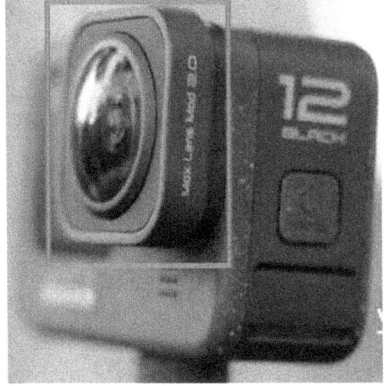

GETTING THE BATTERY CHARGED

To get the battery of your Go Pro 12 charged, follow the steps below:
Ensure that the camera is off and any other accessory attached to it is disconnected

- Pull down the latch on the door handle with the tip of your finger to open the door.

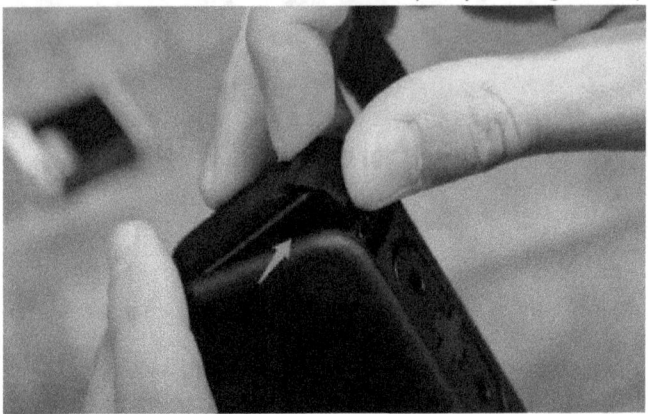

- When the door is opened, connect the USB adapter with the USB cable to the USB port on the camera to start charging

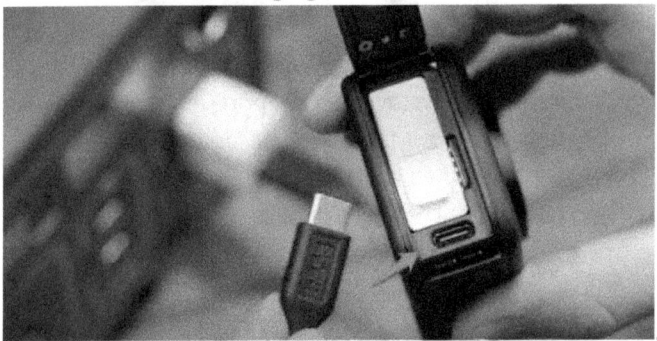

BATTERY MANAGEMENT IN GOPRO HERO 12

Like every device, the battery is the major source of power for the GoPro Hero 12 camera. The camera has delicate parts, including the battery. An important thing to know is that the HERO camera, its battery, and housing are all in one unit. Both the camera and the battery cannot be taken out of their housings.
The battery icon displayed on the camera status screen allows you to monitor your battery status.

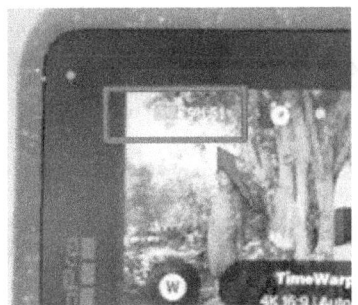

When the battery decreases to 10% or lower, the battery icon blinks. While recording, the camera saves the file and turns off if the battery level hits 0%.

In cases when the battery of your camera drops, you can restore it by charging it with a USB charging adaptor. Using a USB charging adaptor, the battery charges to 80% in about an hour and 100% in about two hours. Of course, the charging rate of the camera is determined by the kind of adaptor that is used. Some chargers may charge more slowly than others. Use only USB chargers with the designation 5V 1A (it is impossible to guarantee the performance of chargers not made by GoPro) or use the provided USB cable to charge the camera from your computer if you are unsure about the voltage and amperage of your charger.

While the camera's battery is being charged, you can still take pictures and videos. Using the supplied USB cable, connect the camera to a USB power source but it is imperative to know that your HERO cannot be operated while it is being charged via a computer.

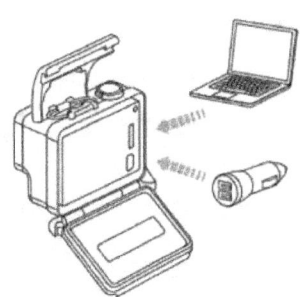

The below are effective tips for handling your battery for optimal function.

- Ensure to power off your camera while charging. This helps it to charge faster.
- Keep your camera away from extreme cold or heat. Temperature extremes can briefly shorten battery life or briefly interfere with the camera's functionality.

- When operating the camera, try to avoid sudden changes in temperature or humidity because condensation could form on the camera or inside of it.
- Do not operate your HERO camera while it is being charged via a computer.
- Never use an external heat source, such as a hair dryer or microwave, to dry the camera or the battery.
- If your camera (inside the housing) gets wet, do not switch it on. Turn off your camera right away if it's already on. Before using the camera once more, let it completely dry.

INSERTING AND REMOVING THE MICROSD CARDS

First and foremost, you need to know that not all SD cards can work on Go Pro Hero 12, and more of a reason you need to know the certain requirements to be on the lookout for when selecting an SD card for your device.

The Go Pro Hero 12 camera is compatible with microSD, microSDHC, and microSDXC with at least 32GB capacity. You must use a video speed class of V30, a UHS speed class of UHS-1, and a write speed of at least 30 MB/s

Inserting the MicroSD Card

- Pull down the latch on the door handle with the tip of your finger to open the door
- When the door is opened, insert the SD card in the card slot with the memory card label facing the battery compartment

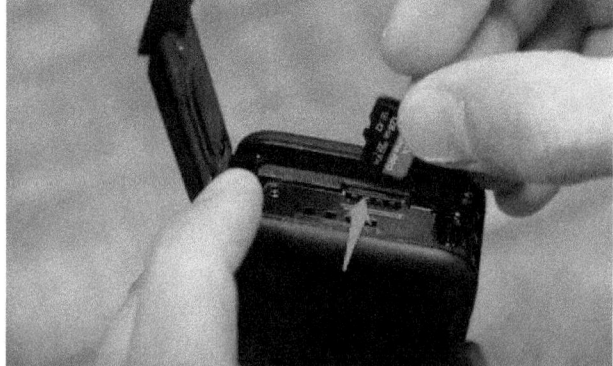

- Use your nail to push the SD card until it fits in properly

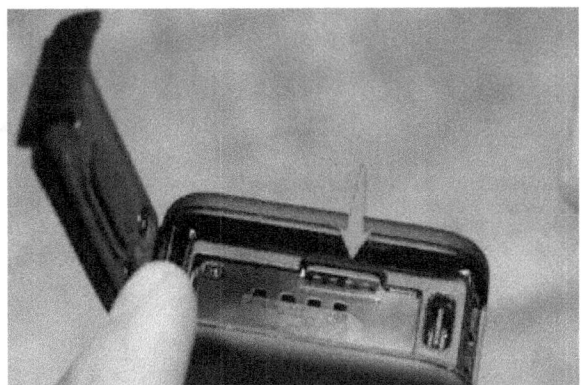

Removing the MicroSD Card

To remove the SD card from your camera, use your nail to push the SD card and release

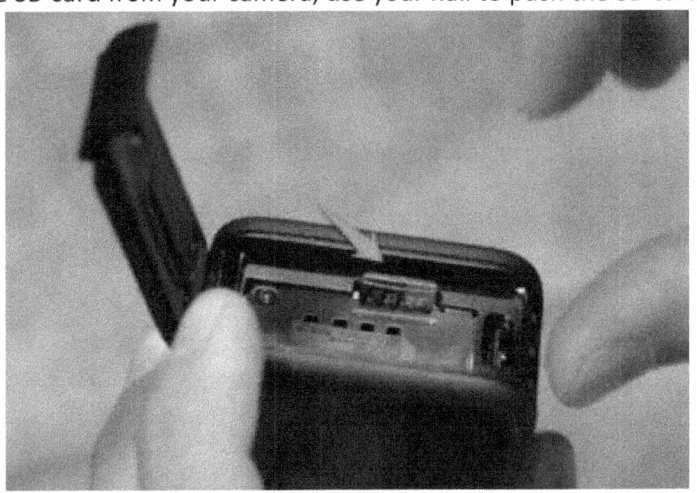

Note:

- It is advisable to turn off your device before inserting and removing the SD card
- Keep the SD card away from liquid substances, dust, and debris.

TURNING YOUR CAMERA ON AND OFF

To power on your camera

- Press the Power Mode button.

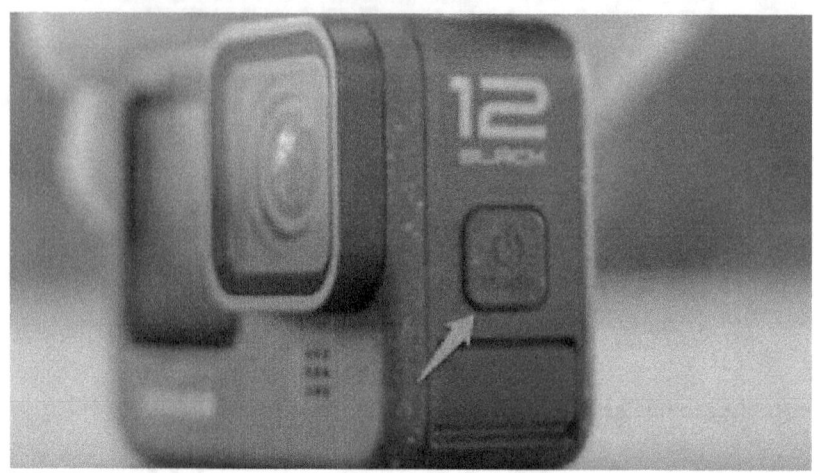

- Here, the status light flashes three times with the sound indicator producing three beeps.
- Here, certain information is displayed on the status screen, which signifies that the camera is powered on

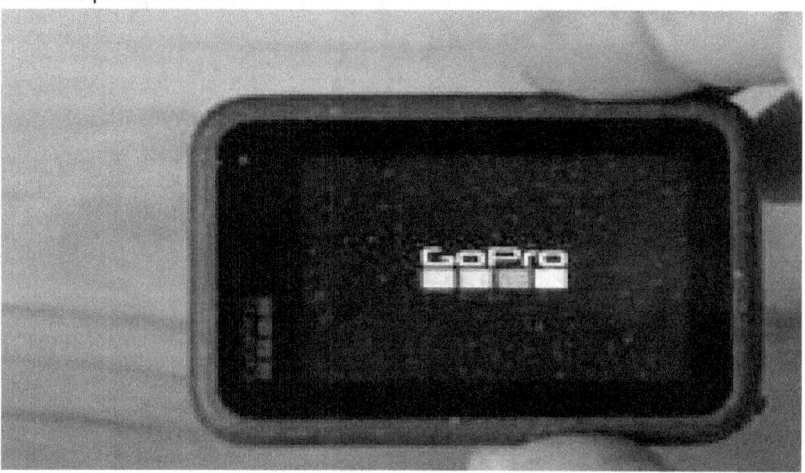

To power off your camera
- Press and hold the Power Mode button for two seconds.
- Here the status light flashes numerous times with the sound indicator producing seven beeps

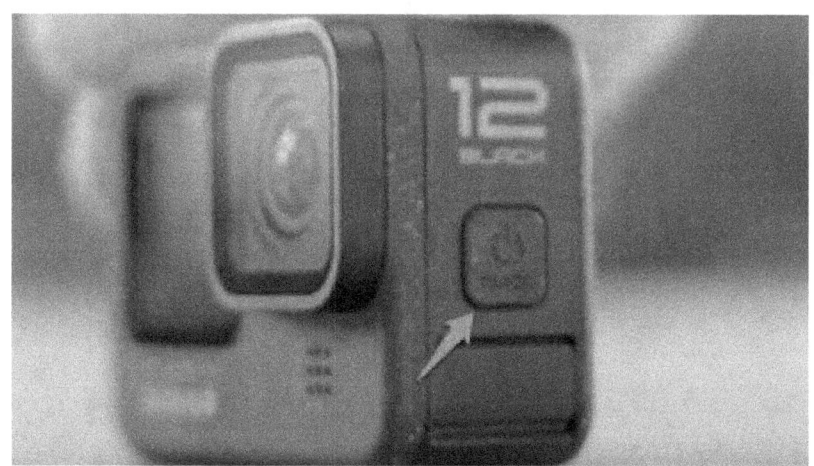

UPDATING THE CAMERA USING THE GOPRO QUICK APP

This is one of the crucial steps to take before you start using your Go Pro Hero 12. To update your camera software using the Go Pro Hero 12, follow the steps below:

- Turn on your camera by long pressing the side button (**Power/Mode**)
- When the screen comes up select the preferred language which is **English**

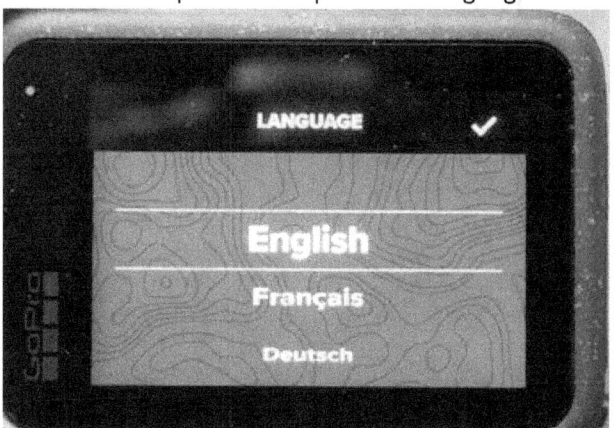

- Select **Agree** on the screen to accept the Gro Pro Hero **Legal Stuff**

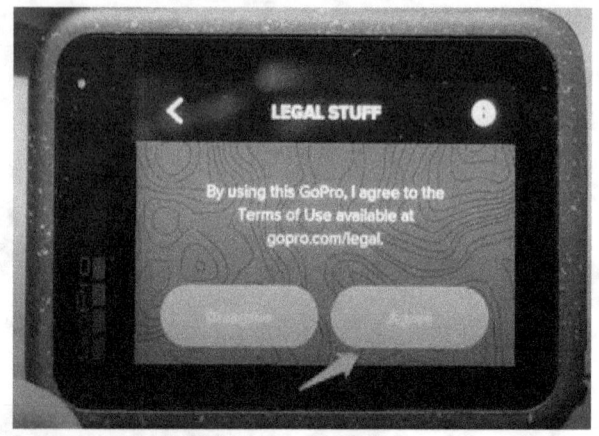

- On the **Voice Control** pop-up menu, select **On**

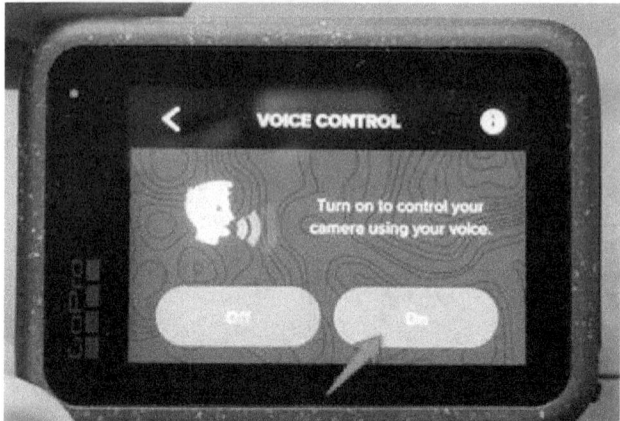

- On the **Voice Control Language** pop-up menu, click on **Confirm** to validate the previously selected language

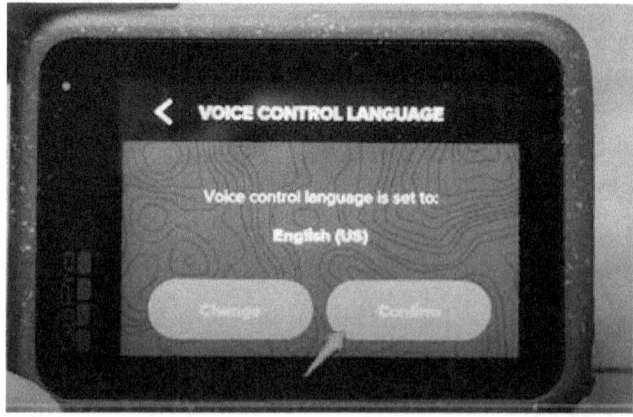

- Here, a menu pops up telling you to connect the Go Pro Quick App via your phone or leave your camera and follow the app instructions.

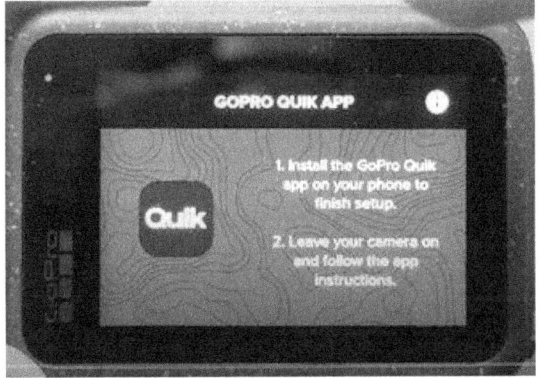

- Pick up your phone and download the Go Pro Quick App with iPhone or Android. Then open the app on your phone
- When the app is opened, click on the upper left-hand button to add a new camera

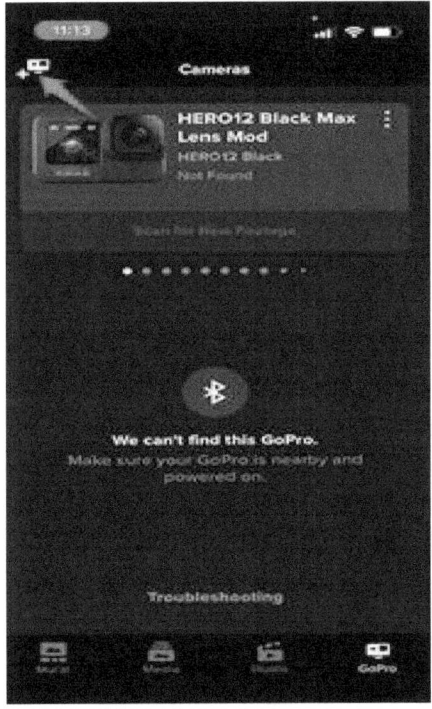

- In the next pop-up screen, click on **Connect Camera** to get your camera connected

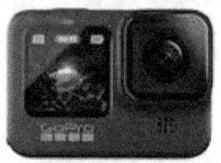

HERO12 Black

We found your GoPro.

Let's get started and connect your GoPro
to your iPhone.

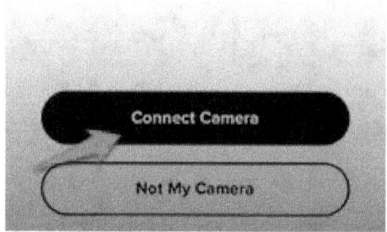

Connect Camera

Not My Camera

- Here, your GoPro requests for a Bluetooth pairing with your phone. Click on **Pair** to validate the request

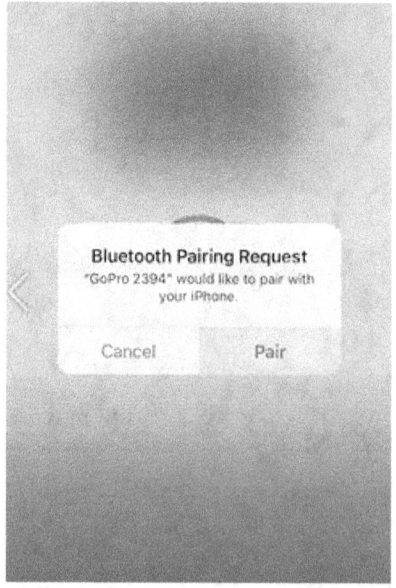

Bluetooth Pairing Request

"GoPro 2394" would like to pair with
your iPhone.

Cancel   Pair

After this, your Camera is successfully paired with your phone

Camera Paired

In the next pop-up window, you can choose to rename your GoPro or leave it as the default name

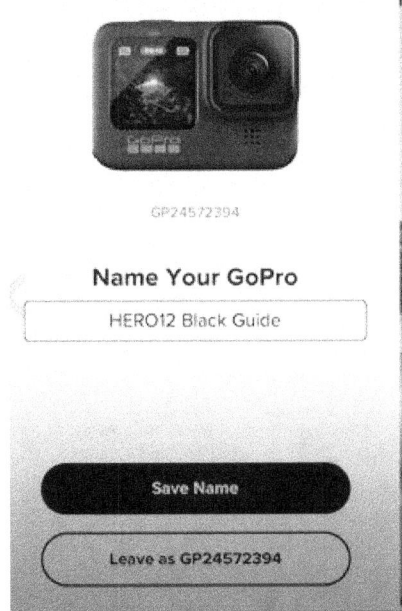

GP24572394

Name Your GoPro

HERO12 Black Guide

Save Name

Leave as GP24572394

- Here, you will be asked to connect to a Wi-Fi network to upload your footage to the cloud and the highlight videos created for you. You can choose to ignore or accept.

- After this is successfully done, click on **Let's Go**
- In the next window that comes up, the screen displays " **A firmware update is available**". Click on **Install Update** to get it installed on your camera

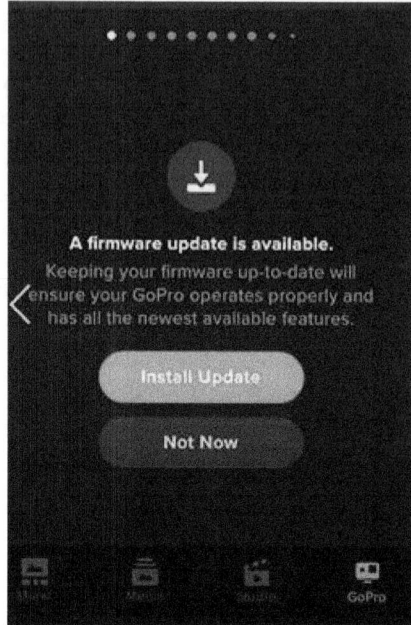

- In the next screen, the firmware update begins to install itself automatically

Update Camera

Installing Update

Don't Go Anywhere!
Do not exit the GoPro Quik app or turn off
your camera during this process.

- Don't leave the app. Your GoPro will power off and on a few times.
- When the update is complete, your camera screen will return to normal.

- After successfully updating the firmware, the camera powers on by itself with a display that shows **Update Complete**

THE CAMERA STATUS SCREEN

When your camera status screen comes, it pops up certain information about the modes and settings of your Go Pro Hero 12.
The following are displayed on your GoPro Hero 12 status screen

- **Mode**: This is the icon that displays the current mode of your camera; video, photo, or time lapse.

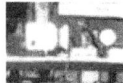

- **Battery Life Percentage**: This is the icon that shows your camera's current battery level

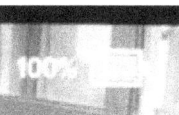

- **Micro SD Card:** This shows the amount of space left on the microSD card

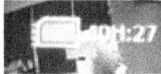

- **Slo Motion:** This is used to select the highest resolution for the chosen slow-mo speed

- **Frame button**: This is the icon used to adjust the framing of your camera such as vertical or full frame

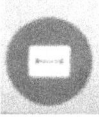

- **Video Mode Quality Button:** This is used to adjust the quality of your video from basic, standard, or highest mode

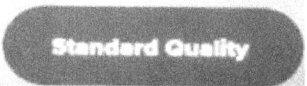

- **The Digital Lens Button:** This icon allows you to set the lens of your camera by selecting from 12 different options available. This icon has the W symbol

Below is the image of the camera status screen.

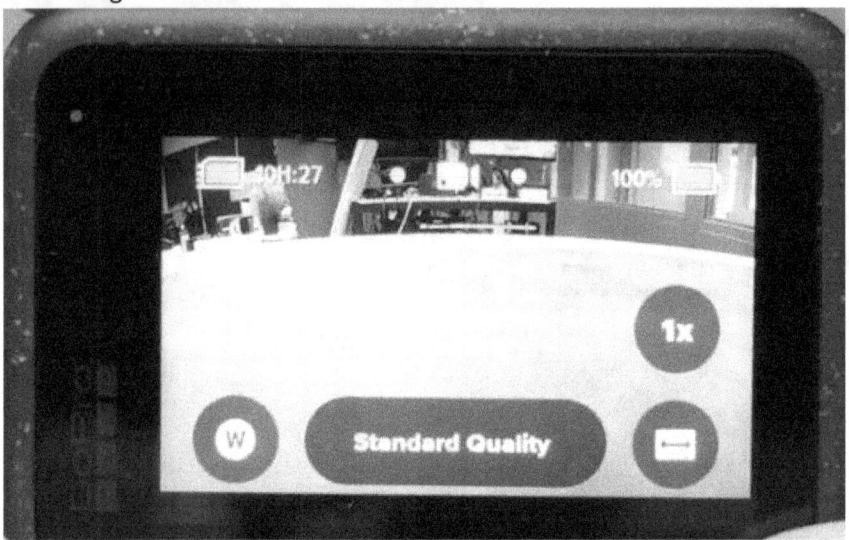

THE GOPRO HERO 12 CAMERA MODES

The GoPro Hero 12 comes with three camera modes which are **Video, Photo,** and **Time Lapse** as seen in the image below: To access the camera modes, press the Power/Mode button severally. You can also swipe left or right to access the different camera modes on your status screen

- **Video (Default):** This is used to record video and this is the default mode of the camera when the camera status screen comes up.
- **Photo**: This is the mode that allows you to capture images or photos
- **Time Lapse**: This is the mode that allows you to take or capture an image every 0.5 seconds.

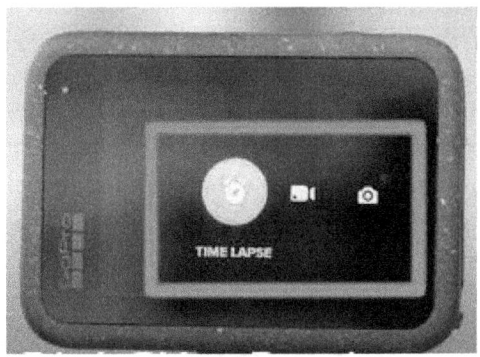

THE GOPRO HERO 12 SETTINGS

The GoPro Hero 12 comes with a lot of options in its settings that can be easily manipulated to get the needed result. In your GoPro, the major settings people use most often the Video, Photo, and Protune
To locate the settings:

- Press the **Mode** button to select the mode you wish to use
- Press the **Up** or **Down** button to circumnavigate through the settings
- Press the **Select** button to adjust the settings
- You can also use the **Up** and **Down** button to make changes to the value of the setting
- To confirm the change made, press the **Select** button.

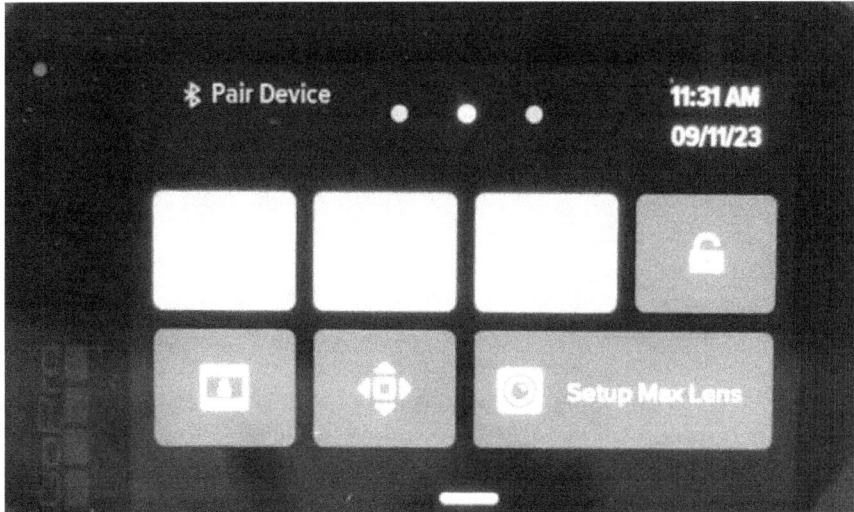

VIDEO MODE: CAPTURING VIDEO USING YOUR GOPRO HERO 12

One of the major things done with GoPro Hero is to make videos or footage. To make video using your GoPro, you need to be sure that your camera mode is set to Video mode. To do that, press the **Power/Mode** button until the **Video** mode appears on your status screen. You can also swipe left or right to select the **Video** mode as shown in the image below

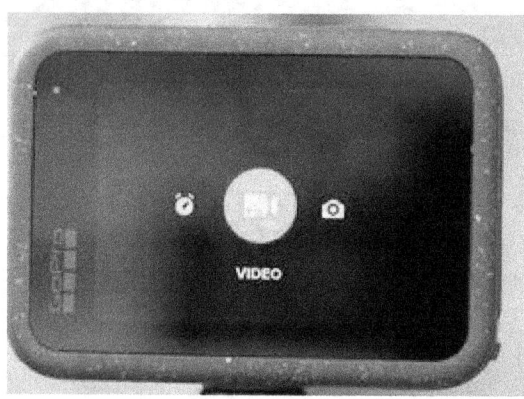

Recording With Your Camera

To start recording, press the Shutter/Select button. Here, the camera makes a beep sound and while the recording is on, the camera status lights flicker.

To Stop Recording With Your Camera

To stop recording, press the Shutter/Select button. Here, the camera status lights flicker thrice and the camera makes three beep sounds to notify you that the recording has stopped.

Note: While recording video with your device, keep note of the following
- Select the appropriate resolution and frame rate
- Use a tripod or mount to keep your device steady and avoid shaky or blur footage
- Use the Hpersmooth feature to give your footage a smooth appearance
- Use a good environment

VIDEO RESOLUTIONS IN GOPRO 12 SETTINGS

The number of horizontal lines in the video is referred to as video resolution (RES). A video that is 1080p, for instance, contains 1080 horizontal lines with a 1920-pixel width per line. More lines and pixels produce clearer and more detailed images. With 1440 lines and a 1920 pixel width per line, a video with a resolution of 1440p is therefore thought to be of higher quality than one with a resolution of 1080p.

Video Resolution	FOV		Screen Resolution/ Aspect Ratio	FPS (NTSC/ PAL)
720p (SuperView)	Ultra Wide		1280X720, 16:9	60/50
720p	Ultra Wide		1280x720, 16:9	60/50
1440p	UltraWide	Quad HD	2560x1440 pixels, 4:3	
1080p	Ultra Wide		1920x1080, 16:9	30/25

- **720p Resolution (Super View):** It is great for images that are taken with the body or equipment attached when you want to record your perspective, and when you need the widest vertical field of view.
- **720p Resolution:** It is great for handheld video of people and slow-motion needs. Most effective at capturing moving targets.
- **1440p:** For body-mounted photos, it is advised to use 1440p resolution compared to 1080p, the aspect ratio of 4:3 captures a wider vertical viewing area. The smoothest, most lifelike outcomes for high-action capture come from high frame rates. fantastic for social media sharing.
- **1080p Resolution:** In order to provide amazing results,1080p, the highest resolution improves clarity and detail.

When deciding the resolution to use for a video recording, you can also consider some of the factors listed below.

- **Field Of View (FOV):** The amount of the scene that can be seen via the camera lens is referred to as the field of view, or FOV, and is expressed in degrees. Narrow FOV just captures a small portion of the scene, whereas Wide FOV captures the most. The FOV selections depend on the resolution and frame rate that are chosen.
  - **Wide:** A large field of vision is advantageous for action photography when you want to fit as much as you can into the frame. Particularly at the scene's edges, this FOV gives the image a fisheye appearance. (If necessary, you may cut that out while editing.)
  - **Medium:** It is a field of view that is in the middle of the scene and has the effect of zooming in on the subject.
  - **Narrow: It is the** narrowest field of view and is very useful for distant content capture. The zooming in on the focal point of the photo has the biggest impact**.**
- **Aspect Ratio:** In the standard Profile, the available aspect ratios for your HERO's video capture are: 16:9 at 1080p, 4:3 at 1440p, 9:16 and 8:7. 16:9 is the standard for televisions and editing software. Although 4:3 footage is 33% taller, it must be

cropped to 16:9 for TV viewing. (Video footage that has not been cropped has black bars around the edges of the image.).

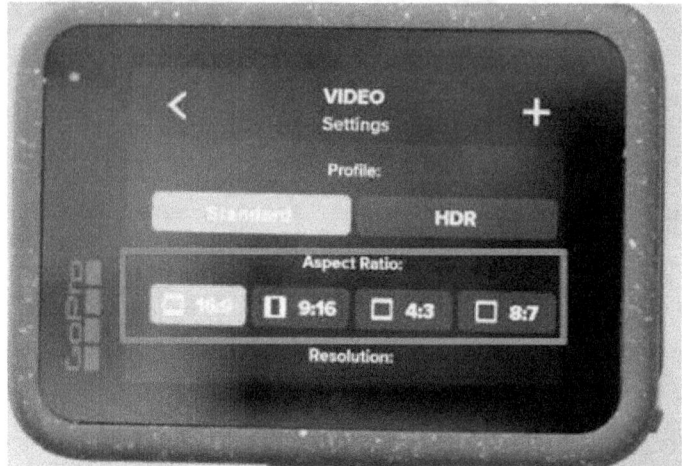

- **Frame Per Seconds (FPS)**: The amount of video frames that are recorded in a second is referred to as frames per second (FPS). Consider the activities you wish to record when choosing a resolution and FPS. Higher resolutions produce more clarity and detail but typically come with lower frame rates. Less clarity and detail are produced at lower resolutions, but greater FPS values can be supported, which are crucial for capturing action. Slow-motion videos can also be produced using higher FPS levels.

Advanced settings in the video mode includes:

- **Video Stabilization (** 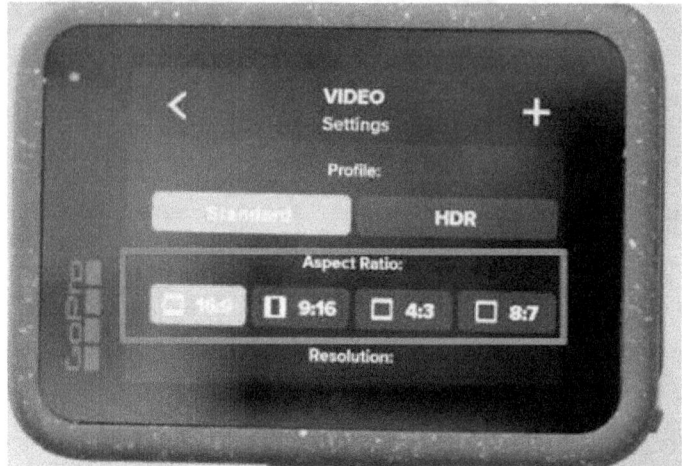 **)**: The footage is offset for motion during capture using this setting. The image is cropped 10% for wide FOV. In particular, footage of sports like cycling, motorcycling, and handheld usage that have relatively modest yet quick motion is smoother as a result. On (the default) is one of the options for this parameter. with Off

- **Auto Low Light (** **)**: You can shoot in low-light situations or when quickly moving in and out of low-light situations using Auto Low Light. To get the optimum exposure and results while shooting at 60 frames per second, the camera will automatically switch to 30 frames per second when it can. This parameter has two possible settings: On (the default) and Off. When both Auto Low Light and Video Stabilisation are enabled and Auto Low Light is activated due to poor lighting, Video Stabilisation is momentarily disabled in order to provide the best image quality in the dim environment.

PHOTO MODE: TAKING PICTURES WITH YOUR GOPRO HERO 12

Another thing you can do with your GoPro device is to take a single photo or burst photos. To take a picture, ensure that the camera mode is set to Photo Mode. To do this, press the **Power/Mode** button until the **Photo** mode appears on your status screen. You can also swipe left or right on the start screen to select the **Photo** mode as shown in the image below

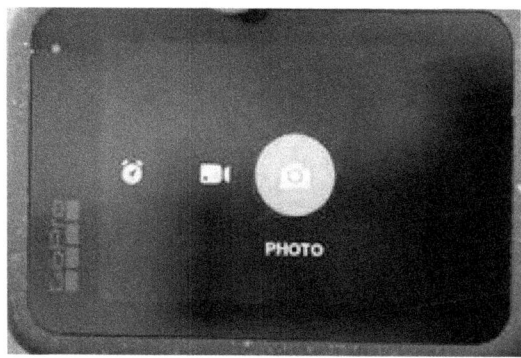

Taking A Single Photo
To take a single photo, swipe the screen **to Photo Mode** and press the **Shutter button** to take a shot. Here, the camera status lights flash, and the counter on the camera status screen increases by one.

Taking Burst Photos
To take burst photos swipe the screen **to Photo Mode** and press and hold the **Shutter button** to take a shot of burst photos. Here, the camera status lights flash, and the counter on the camera status screen increases by ten.

Note: While taking photos with your device, keep note of the following
- Select the appropriate resolution.
- Use a tripod or mount to keep your device steady and avoid shaky or blur footage
- Use the HDR feature to help keep every detail of your photos. HDR means High Dynamic Range.
- Use a good environment

PHOTO RESOLUTIONS FOR GOPRO 12

HERO can take 27.5MP photos in single or continuous bursts. With all advanced settings disabled, Wide is the default Field OF View (FOV) for photos. There are three FOV settings on the camera.

- **Wide**: It is the most expansive field of view. It's advantageous for action shots to fit as much into the frame as feasible. Particularly at the scene's edges, this FOV gives the image a fisheye appearance. (If necessary, you may cut that out while editing.)
- **Medium**: it is a field of view at mid-range and it has the effect of enlarging the focal point of the photograph.
- **Narrow**: It is the smallest field of view with less distortion from fisheye. good for distant content capture. The zooming in on the focal point of the photo is its most notable effect.

The option in the advanced include:

- **Wide Dynamic Range (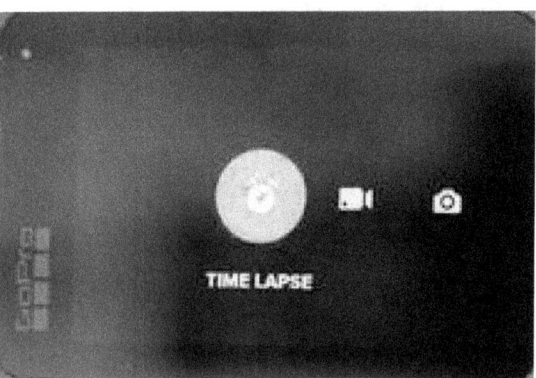)**: With Wide Dynamic Range (WDR), more detail is preserved in both the dark and light portions of an image. A picture that is appropriately exposed for both of these extremes is the end result. When there is backlighting or when there are broad brilliant areas with a dark foreground, this option is extremely helpful.

TIME LAPSE MODE

This is the third mode in the camera mode. This mode allows you to take a shot of several pictures over a specific period and then gather them together to make a video. For instance, you can take shots of several cars with their components and compile them into a video.

You can switch to the Time Lapse Mode following the same steps as the Video and Photo modes.

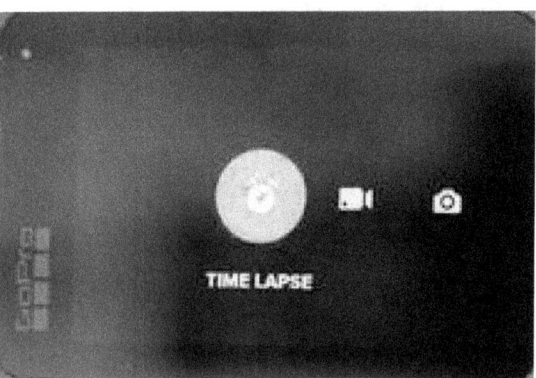

To take pictures using the Time Lapse mode
- Switch the camera mode to Laspes

- Select the interval you wish your GoPro to take photos with. The interval could be 0.5 seconds, 1 second, 2 seconds, etc.
- Then click on the Shutter button for the recording to start. Here the recording will start.

SETTINGS MODES IN GOPRO 12 CAMERA

RESOLUTION: The best image stability and widest field of view are provided by every video, which is recorded at an ultra-wide FOV. When you want to fit as much stuff as you can into the frame, ultra wide FOV works best.

SPOT METER: The Spot meter option is useful for filming in an environment with different lighting from where you are, such as when filming outside while inside a car or in a darkened area while standing in the sun. Spot Metre uses a single spot (⬚)in the center of the image to automatically set the exposure. The Off (the default) and On options are the available settings.

UPSIDE DOWN: The Upside Down option is another settings mode in the GoPro HERO 12 Camera. This setting eradicates the need to flip your video or photographs while editing them after they must have been taken when your camera was placed upside down.

Let`s quickly examine the descriptions of the two options available in the Upisde Down Setting.

- **Up (⬚)**: This implies that the camera is held upright which is always the default state.
- **Down (⬚)**: This implies that the camera is mounted upside down.

QUICKCAPTURE: As the name implies, you may immediately activate your camera with QuikCapture and start taking Time-Lapse pictures or videos. One of the prominent advantages of using QuickCapture is that it helps to save the battery life of the camera. The two possible settings for this one are the On (the default) and Off options.

Do the following to use the Quickcapture option to capture a time-lapsed photo:
- Press and hold the Shutter/Select button for two seconds with the camera off.
- After performing the actions above, your camera starts up automatically and starts taking time-lapse pictures.

Do the following to capture videos using QuickCapture.
- With the camera powered off, press and release the Shutter/Select button.
- Your camera automatically powers on and begins capturing video.

Do the following to stop recording.
- For the camera to turn off and the recording to end, press and hold the Shutter/Select button.

NTSC/PAL: When watching video on a TV or HDTV, frame rates are controlled by the Video Format settings. NTSC/PAL are the two video formats standard generally used.

- **NTSC:** This is the default video format and it views videos in NTSC TV/HDTV
- **PAL:** This video format views videos using PAL/HDTV.

LED: This settings option allows you to choose the camera status light to be used. **Both On (front and rear)** which is the default option, **Both Off**, **Front On,** and **Rear On.**

BEEP: This Setting controls the volume of sound. The volume for the sound indicators can be changed to 100% (the default), 70%, or Off.

DATE/TIME: When you connect your camera to GoPro software, the date and time are automatically set on your camera. If necessary, you can manually set the date and time using this setting.

DELETE: You have the option to remove all files and then format the memory card in this configuration. The LED light beeps to indicate that the deletion is ongoing.

When you choose All/Format, your memory card is formatted and all of the video and photo files on it are removed.

NAVIGATING THROUGH THE SETTINGS

In the settings menu, you can modify settings that apply to all camera modes and change the video resolution.

using the buttons on the camera, you may navigate the settings menu.

Do the following to navigate through the settings Menu:

- To cycle through the Settings mode, continually press the Power/Mode button. You can also cycle through the options of a setting by using the Power/Mode Button
- To open a setting, use the Shutter/Select button.
- To exit the Settings Mode, click the Power/Mode button until it cycles to EXIT, then press the Shutter/Select button to leave the room.

CONTROLLING GOPRO 12 WITH YOUR VOICE

Aside from manually inputting your commands into the GoPro Hero 12 camera, you can also control it using your voice. Although distance, wind, and noisy environments could affect voice Control performance. It is most effective nearby.

To take pictures or videos, your camera does not need to be in a certain mode. The action commands are available in every mode. Depending on the settings you previously chose, your camera takes pictures or videos. With voice control, there are two different sorts of commands available:

- **Action commands**: This enables instantaneous photo or video capturing. For instance, you don't need to switch modes if you just finished recording a video and want to take a picture or start a time-lapse.
- **Mode Commands**: If you want to quickly choose a mode and then use the Shutter button to take a picture, mode commands can be helpful.

Listed below are some action commands and a description of the actions they carry out.

Mode Commands	Performance
"GoPro Time Lapse"	changes the camera's mode to that of the most recent time-lapse session, but does not initiate time-lapse.
"GoPro Video Mode"	transforms the camera's mode to Video (but still doesn't record video).
"GoPro Photo Mode"	switches the camera's mode to Photo mode, but doesn't take pictures until asked to.
"GoPro Burst Mode"	Activates the Burst mode on the camera (but does not take burst images).
Action Commands	Performance
"GoPro start recording"	begins filming a scene.
"GoPro stop recording"	stops video recording.
"GoPro turn off"	turns the camera off.
"GoPro take a photo"	takes a single picture.
"GoPro start time lapse"	starts the time-lapse recording.
"GoPro stop time lapse"	stops the time-lapse camera.
"GoPro shoot burst"	captures photographs in bursts.
"GoPro HiLight"	during recording, it adds a HiLight Tag to the video.

Do the following to activate voice control on GoPro Hero 12.

- Swipe downward from the home screen, then tap on this icon;
- Select an option by tapping **Preferences** > On **Camera Voice Control**.
  Note: *The Preferences menu also allows you to activate or deactivate Voice Control.*
- Change the voice control language if this is the first time you have activated voice control.
- Choose a command from the voice commands listed above.
- On the home screen, slide down and tap to manually disable Voice Control.
- When your camera shuts off, Voice Control likewise goes out of operation.

Do the following to change voice control language.
- Swipe down from the main screen.
- In the Voice Control section, select **Preferences** > **Language**.
- Then select your desired language.

TRANSFERRING AND PLAYING FILES ON GOPRO HERO 12

Your content can be viewed on a computer, TV, smartphone, or tablet in addition to the touch screen on the camera. The microSD card can also be immediately inserted into a gadget, like a computer or compatible TV, to play back material. With this technique, playback resolution is determined by the device's resolution and its capacity to playback that resolution.

Do the following to playback content on your Hero 12 camera.
- Right-swipe to access the gallery (It could take a while for your microSD card to load if it has a lot of data on it.)
- Examine the thumbnails one by one.
  The thumbnail for the photo series (Burst, Time Lapse, and Continuous Pictures shows the first picture in the collection.
- To see a movie or image in full-screen mode, tap on it.
- Tap to include a HiLight Tag, Finding the greatest videos and pictures to share is simple with HiLight Tags.
- Tap to go back to the thumbnail view,
- Swipe down to close the gallery.

To save a scene in a video file as a screenshot in your Hero 12, do the following.
- After opening the gallery with a swipe to the right, press the video that contains the clip you wish to save.
- To start playing the video, tap the **Play** icon,
- Tap the **Pause** icon, [**II**] once you've located the frame you wish to save.
- Tap to screenshot that video frame.
- To choose the frame, if necessary, slide the bar at the bottom of the screen.
- Tap the **Done** icon, then the original video clip remains unaltered and the frame is saved as a snapshot.

Do the following to playback/view your content on your mobile device.
- Use the GoPro app to connect your camera.
- To play back your footage on your smartphone or tablet, use the controls in the app.

You must transfer your video and photo files to a computer before your computer will be able to play them back. Before you can transfer and play files, you must be sure to have installed GoPro software on your PC.

- Connect your camera to your PC using a USB cord.
- Turn the camera on and transfer the documents to your computer or an external hard drive.
- Make use of the GoPro software to play back the files.

Another method to transferring your files out of your camera into your computer is using a card reader. Follow the instructions below to do so

- Be sure the files from your camera have been transferred to an SD card.
- Insert the SD card into a card reader, then connect the card reader to your computer.
- Then you can now transfer your files from the SD card to your computer.

CONNECTING THE HERO 12 CAMERA WITH AN HDTV

Connecting your camera to an HDTV allows you to view and playback your video and photo files in a magnified view. You may view your stuff directly from your camera on a big screen by playing back videos and photographs on your HDTV. This is made possible by a micro HDMI cable. HDMI playback is certified up to 1080p resolution, depending on the device.

- Launch the camera.
- Select **Media** from **Preferences** > **HDMI Output**.
- To connect a camera's HDMI connection to an HDTV, use a micro HDMI cable. On your TV, select the **HDMI input**.
- To cycle among the controls, use the **Mode** button [🔲], and to choose a control, press the **Shutter** button [🔘].
- Press the **Mode** button to go and then continually press the Shutter button to cycle through each thumbnail.
- Tap [⤢] to launch a file in full-screen mode.

Not only can you view your files on an HDTV, but also can you capture videos and photos with your camera using an HDTV.

Do the following to use an HDTV to see the live preview of your camera`s recording.

- Launch the camera.
- Under **Preferences**, select **HDMI Output**, then select **Live**.

- The icons and overlays that you typically see on your touch display will not be there when the preview is displayed on your HDTV.
- To connect a camera's HDMI connection to an HDTV, use a micro HDMI cable. On your TV, select the HDMI input.
- To begin and end recording, press the camera's **Shutter** button.

THE CAMERA HOUSING

The camera housing is packed with two types of backdoors and they are Standard Backdoor and Skeleton Backdoor.

- **The Standard Backdoor**: The housing is watertight to 131' (40m) when using the Standard Backdoor. When you need to shield the camera from elements such as water, sand, dirt, and other pollutants, use this door. Note that the standard is waterproof

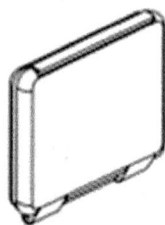

- **The Skeleton Backdoor**: This backdoor is non-waterproof. Better sound quality is achieved by allowing more sound to pass through the Skeleton Backdoor and into the camera's microphone. Additionally, when placed on helmets, motorcycles, bikes, and other fast-moving vehicles, it minimizes wind noise at speeds up to 100 mph. Use this backdoor only if there is no risk of water damage, excessive dirt or dust, or sand accumulation. It is also advised to use this backdoor when driving.

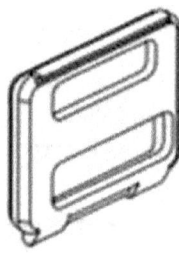

Your HERO camera's backdoor can be changed to accommodate your activity and the shooting environment.

- Open the housing's back door so that it drapes downward.

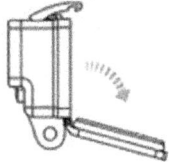

- Until the backdoor snaps free from the frame, forcefully pull it downward. primary structure.

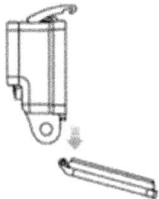

- Position the new backdoor so that it fits into the hinge opening.

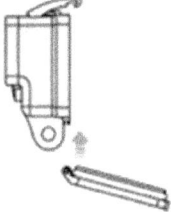

- Push the backdoor upward until it clicks into position.

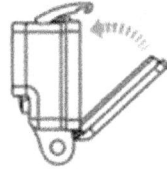

HOW TO PREVENT YOUR CAMERA FROM WATER DAMAGE

If you don't follow these instructions every time you use your GoPro, leaks could occur and harm or wreck your camera. Both the camera and the battery will be harmed by water, which could result in an explosion or fire. Inaccurate user-caused water damage is not covered by your warranty. Do the following to prevent your camera from water damage.

- Your HERO is shielded from water by the rubber seal that lines the Standard Backdoor, creating a waterproof barrier. Keep the rubber seal on the Standard Backdoor clean. Your camera may suffer harm from a leak brought on by a single hair or sand grain.
- Close the Standard Backdoor firmly after each time it has been used in salt water, then rinse and dry the camera housing's exterior with fresh water. Failure may eventually result from salt accumulation in the seal and corrosion of the hinge pin if this is not done.
- Remove the seal from the backdoor, give it a good rinse in fresh water, and then shake it dry—drying with a cloth could weaken the seal. Put the seal back into the Standard Backdoor's grooves.

WORKING WITH THE CAMERA MOUNTS AND LOCKING PLUGS

Depending on the mount you're using, you'll need a Quick Release Buckle, a thumb screw, or other hardware to secure your HERO camera to it.

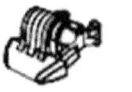 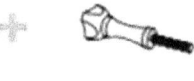

Quick Release Buckle   Thumb Screw

The constructed camera housing can be snapped on and off the locked *Curved Adhesive Mount* or *Flat Adhesive Mount* using the Quick Release Buckle, making it simple to connect the camera to curved and flat surfaces of helmets, automobiles, and other equipment.

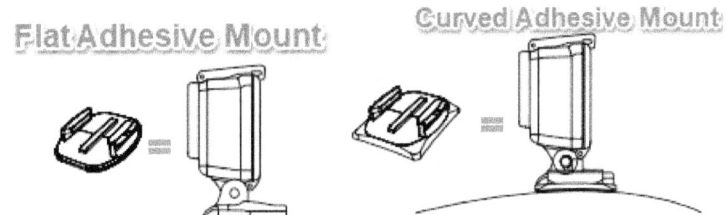

Flat Adhesive Mount

Curved Adhesive Mount

When mounting mounts, adhere to the following rules:

- At least 24 hours before usage, attach the adhesive mounts. To ensure perfect adherence, give it 72 hours.
- Adhesive mounts must only be installed on flat surfaces.
- Surfaces with pores or texture prevent a strong connection from forming. Apply the mount firmly, making sure it covers the entire surface, and press it into place.
- Adhesive mounts should only be used on clean surfaces. Debris such as wax, grease, dirt, or other substances weaken the binding and increase the chance of losing the camera if the connection breaks.
- In a temperature-controlled environment, attach adhesive mounts.
- If adhesives are applied to cold or moist surfaces, they will not adhere well.
- Always choose a helmet that complies with the relevant safety standards if you plan to use your camera with a GoPro helmet mount or strap. Make sure the helmet you choose fits you properly and is the appropriate size for the sport or activity you intend to engage in.
- Make sure your helmet is in good shape by giving it a once-over, and use it safely by adhering to the manufacturer's recommendations. Any helmet that has taken a significant beating has to be replaced. No helmet can guarantee safety from harm in every collision.

Use the locking plug to firmly lock the Quick Release Buckle fingers into place if you're using the HERO in high-impact sports like surfing or skiing where a large amount of impact could happen. The locking plug aids in preventing unintentional mounting release of the housing.

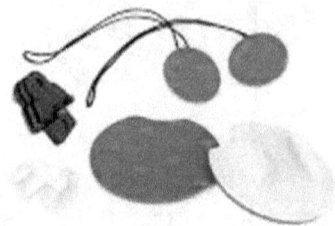

Do the following to attach a locking plug:

- Wrap the thumbscrew with the circular ring. The ring around the locking plug serves as a leash to keep it from falling or being misplaced.
- When it clicks into position, slide the Quick Release Buckle into the mount.
- Insert the U-shaped portion of the plug into the Quick Release Buckle's U-shaped opening.

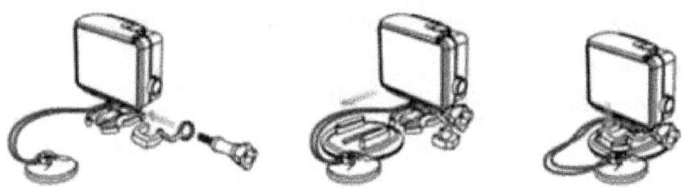

IMPORTANT MESSAGES TO TAKE NOTE OF WHEN USING YOUR HERO CAMERA

Below are some important messages to pay attention to when using a Hero camera

- **FILE REPAIR ICON**: The file repair icon signifies a corrupted file for the most recent recording. Any button can be clicked to repair the file.

- **TEMPERATURE ICON**: Because the Hero camera is built to recognize overheating situations and to react appropriately, the Temperature icon shows on the camera status screen when the camera gets too hot and has to cool down. Just wait for it to cool off before attempting to use it again. Your camera was built to recognize overheating situations and to react appropriately.

- **NO SD**: No card is present, according to this statement. To take pictures and movies, the camera needs a microSD, microSDHC, or microSDXC card.
- **FORMAT SD?**: This indicates that the card is either not formatted or is prepared incorrectly. You can either choose Yes to format the card or No to insert a different card. Choosing YES will result in the deletion of all files on the card.
- **FULL**: This message signifies that the card is full and should be replaced with a card with more space or some files should be deleted from the already filled card to relieve it of space.
- **SD ERR**: This signifies that the card cannot be read.

CONCLUSION

If you are reading this chapter of the book, you have finished the user guide. I must express my gratitude for your tenacity and the effort you put forth to see this through to its very end.

You have surely been able to learn more as an experienced learner and new things as a beginner. Even if this hasn't been finished yet, you can study more and improve your GoPro HERO 12 skill online.

Remember to distribute this user guide to your friends, family, coworkers, and business associates.